Laconic Poetry & Prose

Printed in the United States of America

First Printing, 2023

ISBN 979-8-218-19456-7

Cover Design by Tiffany Robinson

Amazon Kindle Direct Publishing

410 Terry Ave N

Seattle, WA 98109

To My Parents

Francis Williams
&
George Jackson

Thank you for
creating the creator

I am grateful!

LACONIC
/luh-kon-ik\

USING FEW WORDS; EXPRESSING MUCH
IN FEW WORDS; CONCISE

Laconic Poetry & Prose

1

Be unrestrained
Go Forward
Don't Fall
Don't Fail

Conquer!

Eliza Williams

Laconic Poetry & Prose

2

Life is beautiful
because you get to see it but
you don't get to keep it
Life is but a dream!
Think on your feet and not
on your knees

Eliza Williams

Laconic Poetry & Prose

3

When I am at spring
I am at peace
I am still like the tree that breathes
I am alive like a body that bleeds
I am the flower that grows the seed
I am the reason for
EVE

Eliza Williams

Laconic Poetry & Prose

4

Unsuccessful
Unfulfilled
Unloved
Untouched
Unhappy
Untraveled
She needs to UN-ravel, the fault in her stars
She will then outshine light itself

Eliza Williams

Laconic Poetry & Prose

5

We are all masquerading
We are all pretending to be happy when we are being controlled
We cannot be happy when we are being told
Perhaps, money is the only thing that is truly happy
It dictates where you go
where you sleep
what you eat
what you wear
For some, it dictates their state of happiness and unhappiness
There is no such thing as financial freedom because even freedom costs
Break Out!
Break Out!
Break Out!

Eliza Williams

6

Let me see all of you
undress
Let me see all of you
No lies
only naked truth
Tell me what you will and won't do
Give me your pain
Give me your past
Give me your regrets and your shame
Give me your love and desire
Give me your delightful peace
I promise to give you all of me

Eliza Williams

Laconic Poetry & Prose

7

I am seeing with the eye of a telescope
Listening to the rain pour
Purple haze dancing on my lips
Dutch in between my tips
Hearing the moans
Oh the passion it takes to touch
I feel loved in my nakedness in this room alone

Eliza Williams

8

It's a shame that miscommunication
can happen if one ____ is out of place.

Eliza Williams

Laconic Poetry & Prose

9

"If I just take this make-up off
I would like myself so much
better," she said.

Hug yourself
Love yourself
You are a gem
No one can love you like you can

Eliza Williams

Laconic Poetry & Prose

10

Sometimes I feel
I'm doing too much
and not
enough

Eliza Williams

Laconic Poetry & Prose

11

I have to let go of anger because it burns
I have to let go of hurt because it aches
I have to let go of pain because it bleeds me heavy
I have to let go of sadness because it weighs me down like quicksand
I have to purge all things I don't need
I have to drink purified waters
I have to be bold enough to cross borders
I have to learn to put me first
I have to fulfill my purpose purposefully
It's ok for me to love myself selfishfully
so that I may give to myself unselfishfully
I cannot let people drain me of my energy
I must respect the law of reciporcity
But above all, I must love all of me

Eliza Williams

Laconic Poetry & Prose

12

Heard a voice that said let darkness in
I said darkness is not my friend
Please don't ever come by again
I'm practicing the power of Zen

Eliza Williams

Laconic Poetry & Prose

13

I'm present in my past
Every moment I see don't seem to last
My future demands my presence
I have been neglecting my health
blocking access to abundant wealth
I need rest
I won't make it
if I'm underneath this
amount of stress
Bless the night
Family can sometimes be the best

Eliza Williams

Laconic Poetry & Prose

14

I've let go but you still got a hold on me
I'm still fighting for what you are and what I
thought you to be

Eliza Williams

Laconic Poetry & Prose

15

Some days I've wanted to be dead but
I have never desired to kill
myself

Eliza Williams

Laconic Poetry & Prose

16

I lost my mind
Yes! I lost my mind
It was necessary
I have surrendered to new beginnings
and made space for happy endings
I have detached from past programming
and here I'm still standing

Eliza Williams

17

I know that I must dispel all judgment of me
Even the judgment I want to keep
I know that I must clip my weeds and water my seeds
I know that must surrender if I want this peace
I know that I must surrender to EVERYTHING peace
OHM!

Eliza Williams

18

Please don't be threatened by the woman your mind
has made of me
For I'm just a girl underneath
It is the girl that has given birth to the woman you see
The girl only made the woman she needs

Eliza Williams

Laconic Poetry & Prose

19

You are my wind
I take you as you come and go
When you are away save some for me
Fleeting is your breeze
You give me high lows and low highs
Oh give rise
Take me away with you when you decide to leave
Take me on a trip beyond the sea and beneath the trees
Dear wind free the captive in me
I long to be wherever the wind blows
Come wind

Eliza Williams

Laconic Poetry & Prose

20

I have a disconnect in my mental wires
Illusive thoughts run my mind rampant until they decide to expire
Some days I'm so exhausted by my thoughts that I have no
motivation to fulfill my desires
I tire
Lord knows I tire
I need stitches
to patch up these systematic glitches
I don't want to do this alone
but I know I have to endure this until I can make
my mind my home

Eliza Williams

Laconic Poetry & Prose

21

I finally understand why the
elderly said "never suffer twice!" You worry before
you know the facts in that which you are worried
about

Eliza Williams

Laconic Poetry & Prose

22

Laughter is healing me
when I am laughing I cannot
think a thing

Eliza Williams

Laconic Poetry & Prose

23

I'm looking at the trees
Feeling the breeze
Spending my time with those
that love me

Eliza Williams

Laconic Poetry & Prose

24

Sometimes it is the
pleasure in the pain that
brings you so much shame

Eliza Williams

Laconic Poetry & Prose

25

Porn is not my reality although I
relish in its world of fantasy
It is only I who knows of my sexual insanity

Eliza Williams

Laconic Poetry & Prose

26

There should be
no guilt
in pleasure

Eliza Williams

27

I apologize if you feel
forced but I can lend no
apology for my being a
force

Eliza Williams

28

I cannot
repent if
I don't
know
sin

Eliza Williams

Laconic Poetry & Prose

29

I am a stream of water with
two sides
One side is still and the other side flows
without limitation
It is the still that has made way for the flow

Eliza Williams

30

Covid-19/Coronvirus
Cardi-B said "this shit is getting real!" I wonder
if it's even real
Some of us are dying and some us are
being killed
Here a strand
there a strand
Strands everywhere
and it just emerged out of thin air
holding us all captive sometimes killing the
elderly
children
woman
and
man

Eliza Williams

Laconic Poetry & Prose

31

Lies are
burgeoning
burdens
Truths are limitless
liberations

Eliza Williams

Laconic Poetry & Prose

32

I am a floating cloud with
no particular origin
I live without concerns
of where I'm from
I never die
However I do take on many forms
Each day I am reborn

Eliza Williams

Laconic Poetry & Prose

33

My vision is 20/40
It means I can't see far
but who needs to see when it is a
present to just be where you are

Eliza Williams

Laconic Poetry & Prose

34

It takes courage to examine yourself
closely in a world where people
are taught to hide from themselves

Eliza Williams

35

Black Lives Matter
so I'm told
I can't seem to keep
up with the black death
toll
Do I stay or do I go
Oh
takers of black life
what do you propose

Eliza Williams

Laconic Poetry & Prose

36

Sometimes you got to
say fuck you to keep
your balance
#middlefinger

Eliza Williams

Laconic Poetry & Prose

37

Never be afraid of the
unknown
for
this is your time
to create knowing

Eliza Williams

38

In this country
after
500
600
years
I find myself crying
recycling my ancestors tears

Rest In Peace
to the black lives
that did not matter to people who
don't believe that black life is a matter

Eliza Williams

Laconic Poetry & Prose

39

I sayless to say more
The quieter I am the more people
want to hear from me
but my objective is to be heard
not
speak

Eliza Williams

Laconic Poetry & Prose

40

Be kind to every human for you
cannot know how their spirit is
experiencing
their flesh

Eliza Williams

Laconic Poetry & Prose

41

It is not in my nature to be human
for
I am experiencing
human as a spiritual being

Eliza Williams

Laconic Poetry & Prose

42

If one cannot rejoice in living
longer
then one has already chosen death
in this life

Eliza Williams

43

Shame on us adults taking the child
from the children
We take fun out of the building

Eliza Williams

44

If it does not involve hurting people then
I stand for the cause
for
we are just
hurt people after all

Eliza Williams

Laconic Poetry & Prose

45

There are some days
I desire to be a child again
Those are also the days I realize
I have failed at nurturing
the child
within

Eliza Williams

46

It is a sad thing to be
grounded in something
that cannot possibly bring one freedom

Eliza Williams

Laconic Poetry & Prose

47

Give only because you have
Giving needs no reciprocity

Eliza Williams

Laconic Poetry & Prose

48

Peace is freedom's equivalent
If I am at peace then I am free

Eliza Williams

Laconic Poetry & Prose

49

Inner peace
is
my
only destination in
this life

Eliza Williams

Laconic Poetry & Prose

50

With this courage
I will haunt my
fears

Eliza Williams

51

In America
everything is for sale
Even
human
bodies
water
dirt
and
trees
I am 35 years young and this is something
that still perplexes me
Why can't everybody and everything just be free

Eliza Williams

52

The
devil
is
the
adversary
of self

Eliza Williams

Laconic Poetry & Prose

53

When does a human becomes super
or is it already super to be human

Eliza Williams

Laconic Poetry & Prose

54

The
devil
worships
me

Eliza Williams

55

Momma said "Mom and Daddy can help you with
anything you go through
but if you done got in your head that's
something you have to undo"

Daddy agreed "And remember illusions can't hurt you"

I nodded
knowing there were no lies just the
reign of truth
for they are my makers
if
they don't know
then who

Eliza Williams

Laconic Poetry & Prose

56

I am learning that the mind can go to
infinite amount of spaces
involuntarily
how you respond emotionally to
the thoughts it has generated could make
all the difference
of heaven or hell for you

Eliza Williams

57

If you are feeling guilty about your pleasure
then it is not pleasure
It is the illusion of pleasure
It is your spirit calling out in hopes that you
would understand that it is displeased with your flesh's desire
That is the time you must redirect your attention
to re-alignment of mind body and soul

Eliza Williams

Laconic Poetry & Prose

58

Into me see
Show me all of you
and I'll
show you all of me
Let's get close

Eliza Williams

Laconic Poetry & Prose

59

Let's ascend beyond the characterizations
& classifications of women and men
Let us explore the nakedness underneath
our skin

Eliza Williams

Laconic Poetry & Prose

60

My heart is on
hiatus
Settling is outdated

Eliza Williams

Laconic Poetry & Prose

61

Say it as it is
never stop
the practice of putting words
to the emotions you feel

Eliza Williams

Laconic Poetry & Prose

62

When you feel weak
When you feel defeat
Just remember you have me

Sincerely,
Strength

PS. You are stronger than
you know

Eliza Williams

Laconic Poetry & Prose

63

We live in a society that renders you old
before you are indeed so
Nothing ever stops
Everything is always on the go

Our society is a stillness interference
It disturbs energetic perseverance

Eliza Williams

Laconic Poetry & Prose

64

If you truly love and care for
someone the least and most you
can do for them is communicate

Eliza Williams

Laconic Poetry & Prose

65

09/08/2020
Today I cried…

Eliza Williams

Laconic Poetry & Prose

66

She thinks he's the one
I think she's the one
One of us is wrong

Eliza Williams

67

I'm not always honest about my feelings
This is me currently being honest
about my present feelings
It's timing for me

Eliza Williams

68

If I want to create
something timeless
then I must suspend
the idea of time

Eliza Williams

Laconic Poetry & Prose

69

The change is
happening
too fast
nothing seems
to
last

Eliza Williams

70

A boy once told me that writing
in my journal is the old
way of doing things
Now I wonder whatever did he mean
Is it so
that writing is no
longer a thing

Eliza Williams

Laconic Poetry & Prose

71

This is a message
to my fears
I will NOT let you interfere

Eliza Williams

Laconic Poetry & Prose

72

I'm tired of
connecting
just to
disconnect
I need other
ways to learn
lessons

Eliza Williams

Laconic Poetry & Prose

73

I wish there were
two of me
but then again
there are two of me
One is happy and
one is so sad

Eliza Williams

Laconic Poetry & Prose

74

We are foolish humans
We are
We will fall for
someone's potential
and totally ignore
their deliberate inaction

I am human
Sighs…

Eliza Williams

Laconic Poetry & Prose

75

Is it possible to
be
overwhelmed
by
one's own
abundance

Eliza Williams

Laconic Poetry & Prose

76

Sorry that everything has a
price but I vow
to only charge
you for the value
you put on
your life

Eliza Williams

Laconic Poetry & Prose

77

Choosing not
to
choose
is a
choice to
stay stuck

Eliza Williams

You can have
everything
but
you rather
have it all

Eliza Williams

79

I am reversibly flawed
I have fallen for someone
who cannot catch me
I have assigned value to someone
that they have yet to see in themselves
Perhaps
I have devalued myself

I have opened to someone
who is closed
I have been
obliviously loyal to someone
who has an impossible
inability
to commit

It felt good once
Then it hurt
Then I no longer felt

Then I realized I had the power to release ALL
that was no longer of service to me
#hardlessons

Eliza Williams

Laconic Poetry & Prose

80

I have already
decided that I
want you as
you are
but you've decided
you need to be someone else

Eliza Williams

Laconic Poetry & Prose

81

Which
way
Straight
ahead

Eliza Williams

82

I'm tired of working
for my needs
because I got
shit that
I want

Eliza Williams

Laconic Poetry & Prose

83

I am often accused of
reading into things too deeply
Ironically the accusations come
from those that lack depth
or
those who are afraid of their own depth

Eliza Williams

84

I have never had
trouble being myself
until someone forces
themselves upon me

Eliza Williams

Laconic Poetry & Prose

85

Demons are habitual
until you nuture
what made them demons

Eliza Williams

Laconic Poetry & Prose

86

I can run faster and further
if I just release these chains
Ah
the power restored when one
is unrestrained

Eliza Williams

87

I was once afraid of
becoming something that
I did not recognize
Perhaps
I knew that I was
already something I
did not recognize

Eliza Williams

88

With this pen
I'm not only a
writer
For
I am too
a painter

Eliza Williams

Laconic Poetry & Prose

89

Character stands
above any
amount of
beauty
physically bestowed
upon human
Character is beautiful

Eliza Williams

90

See that girl
her light
cannot
be dimmed
no matter
the inevitable
unwavering
condemn

Eliza Williams

91

Sometimes
it takes walking
out on someone
temporarily
for them
to realize
you are
forever

Eliza Williams

Laconic Poetry & Prose

92

I have this
life of mine
to live
and
no one else

Eliza Williams

93

How can you begin
to heal
if
you do not
allow yourself
to
feel

Eliza Williams

94

Today I did not
vote
and
tomorrow I won't
either
For
I have not the capacity
to believe in neither

#trumporbiden

Eliza Williams

Laconic Poetry & Prose

95

There are times
I wonder
is the
one I'm thinking
about
thinking about
me

Eliza Williams

96

I have relinquished
my nights that led to
impossible drinking
yet
I still can't find
the genesis of this
overthinking

Eliza Williams

97

Rather by a lake
or
the sea
I write the greatest parts of
me
I just listen closely and let
the water speak

Eliza Williams

98

You cannot eat politics
but politics is eating me
I care not who makes
the laws
I just want the
power to decide
what I eat

Eliza Williams

99

A woman's nakedness
is not always a matter
of invitation or attention seeking
Freedom can't be obtained
without nakedness

Eliza Williams

Laconic Poetry & Prose

100

I'm not sure
I can supply
what is being
demanded without
losing my value

Eliza Williams

Laconic Poetry & Prose

101

Permit a
pass
everybody
has a
past

Eliza Williams

Laconic Poetry & Prose

102

I'm not low
so
I have
no desire
to get high

Eliza Williams

Laconic Poetry & Prose

103

What is your
identity
underneath the
identity
you have
forged

Eliza Williams

104

<u>About a girl</u>
She's stuck…
in between mothers
in between brothers
in between lovers
in between covers

Eliza Williams

Laconic Poetry & Prose

105

I had
unaddressed demons
I had to undress and address my demons

Eliza Williams

Laconic Poetry & Prose

106

Confessions
about
affections
that were only
confections

Eliza Williams

107

The world has
become a place of
endless battles
and
endless babble

Eliza Williams

Laconic Poetry & Prose

108

Perhaps you
are not where you
want to be
because you forgot
that journeys
don't have
specific
destinations

Eliza Williams

109

Sometimes I
fast
because
I
hunger for
more than just
food

Eliza Williams

Laconic Poetry & Prose

110

Tell yourself who
you are and who
you are NOT
needs
no discussion

Eliza Williams

Laconic Poetry & Prose

111

Not too much, not too little,
just enough
I'm learning "enough"
Enough is balance

Eliza Williams

Laconic Poetry & Prose

112

You see the most
beautiful
things when
your camera is
NOT
on

Eliza Williams

113

"Whatever would I do without my phone?"
the new generation screamed!
Who knows?
Maybe you could
BE
without it.

Eliza Williams

114

I want to know
how to
survive in
every place
on earth
Adaptation
is
key

Eliza Williams

Laconic Poetry & Prose

115

You can't want change
and not want to do the
work of changing
They are two
sides
of
one coin

Eliza Williams

Laconic Poetry & Prose

116

Sacrifice
overconsumption
for
a purposeful
life

Eliza Williams

117

I don't
know about
you but
I
want to
die living

Eliza Williams

Laconic Poetry & Prose

118

Our society has
been made so
convenient that
even effort seems
overwhelming

Eliza Williams

Laconic Poetry & Prose

119

Dear Black Men

Crying does not make you weak
it is but a release
just like sweat
just like sex
It is but a release
it is a type of therapy
Tears won't make you less to me

Sincerely,
A Black Woman

Eliza Williams

Laconic Poetry & Prose

120

I don't like proving my
worth to others
In fact
I don't believe
worth is a
proving matter

Eliza Williams

Laconic Poetry & Prose

121

Is homosexuality
nature's
population
control?

Relax!!
It's just a passing thought!

Eliza Williams

Laconic Poetry & Prose

122

Have you ever
experienced a
day so good
that you could die
because you've lived

I have! :-)

Eliza Williams

123

If I can be happy
where I am
I can
be happy where
I'm going

Eliza Williams

Laconic Poetry & Prose

124

I'm learning that it's
hard to stay secure
amid so many
changes
Changes give
way to
insecurities

Eliza Williams

Laconic Poetry & Prose

125

I got demons from
my past trying to
come up still
reminding me that
I must do the I-N-G
before I can
say that I
am
healED

Eliza Williams

Laconic Poetry & Prose

126

Who knew self love
came with a price?

It comes with the price of
exterminating everything
and everyone you thought you
loved
And those who you thought loved you
It comes with the price of not being able
to accept anything less than you're worth
Ah, what a beautiful price to pay

Eliza Williams

127

When you take me too fast
I can't trust
that you believe we will last

Eliza Williams

Laconic Poetry & Prose

128

Giving someone the passcode
to your phone is allowing
access into yourself
these days

Eliza Williams

Laconic Poetry & Prose

129

We've been sold on the idea
that we need what we want
We live in a society where we are
so consumed by our wants that
we inadvertently neglect our needs

Eliza Williams

130

I don't mind
the rain
because
I'm a
flower

Eliza Williams

Laconic Poetry & Prose

131

I want to make sure it's
something I want and
not just my body
The flesh can be
so tricky

Eliza Williams

Laconic Poetry & Prose

132

Have you experienced joy
an uncontrollable
happiness
with an overwhelming
outpour

Yes
I have

:-)

Eliza Williams

Laconic Poetry & Prose

133

I will never expect
more than
your best
but I refuse
to let you give
me less

Eliza Williams

Laconic Poetry & Prose

134

Loving yourself
externally
is an internal matter

Eliza Williams

Laconic Poetry & Prose

135

There are
those who
love
and those that
are unloved

Eliza Williams

Laconic Poetry & Prose

136

When I like something
or someone I like to
consume it or them
in large
quantities

Eliza Williams

Laconic Poetry & Prose

137

No matter how bad
I want them for myself
I simply sometimes have to accept
that my only purpose in their life
may be to make them
better for someone else

Eliza Williams

Laconic Poetry & Prose

138

When I'm angry it usually stems from not being
able to control something (or frankly someone)
not being understood
feeling disrespected
or
just not having the words to make
myself understood
When I'm reaching for anger
I have to ask myself important questions

Why do I want to control
Why is it important for me to be understood by
someone else
Why do I care about someone's disrespect if
I respect me enough
Why do I have to have the words in the moment

I like to take my time with me

Eliza Williams

Laconic Poetry & Prose

139

Sometimes I run
from my depth
fearing it's too deep for me
but it's really the fear of sharing
it with someone else
who does not
have capacity

Eliza Williams

Laconic Poetry & Prose

140

I am not afraid to face all
of me sober
I truly love that about myself

Eliza Williams

141

The most dangerous part of
vulnerability is giving yourself
to someone knowing that they
have potential to hurt you in
the greatest way
But if you are to give yourself
you have to be okay with that

Eliza Williams

142

I reject
anything
that is
anti-peace

Eliza Williams

Laconic Poetry & Prose

143

Random
Imagine getting your
body and your face done
post it for the world to see
and not receive a single like

Don't forget to do it for you

Eliza Williams

144

It's good to
know
people in
high
and
low
places

All people are valuable in one
way or another
It's the way we choose
to use them

Eliza Williams

145

One day I'll
be so good
I'll quote myself

Shid if I
don't believe
in me
who will

Eliza Williams

Laconic Poetry & Prose

146

Some days it's easy to
get ahead of yourself with
overthinking
Those are the days to
remember to take things
one day at a time

Eliza Williams

Laconic Poetry & Prose

147

Sometimes I wear
clothes that make me
appear "less attractive" so
the real me can do the attracting

Eliza Williams

Laconic Poetry & Prose

148

Even though
I can
do it alone I
don't want to
be left to do
it alone

Eliza Williams

Laconic Poetry & Prose

149

May I ask
while you were busy
concerning yourself with
your class and seating
did you notice we were being
flown by the same pilot
on the same plane
underneath the same sky

Because I did

Eliza Williams

Laconic Poetry & Prose

150

I experience fleeting feelings of
loneliness
when
I want someone to be here
but
there are times when I cannot
bear to have anyone here

Eliza Williams

Laconic Poetry & Prose

151

I notice I do not
procrastinate
when
my vision
is clear

Eliza Williams

Laconic Poetry & Prose

152

Men tend to be at
war alot
And women
are told
we are chaotic
more often than not
but if I'm comparing we
are way more civil
We are not the ones
doing all that senseless killing

Eliza Williams

Laconic Poetry & Prose

153

Why is it that when
a man wants to
show his peers and
the world he is comfortable
in his sexuality it almost always
result in him
effeminizing
himself

Eliza Williams

Laconic Poetry & Prose

154

Self
expression
is a
lost art

Eliza Williams

155

My
father
is
a trigger
for me

Eliza Williams

Laconic Poetry & Prose

156

We are a
DIY
ass society
No one is interesting
in building anymore
Men and women
have reduced each
other to nothing
but mere transactional
sexual pastime

Eliza Williams

Laconic Poetry & Prose

157

There can
be no
discipline
without
sacrifice

Eliza Williams

Laconic Poetry & Prose

158

I need rest
if I'm
to engage
with
the restless

Eliza Williams

Laconic Poetry & Prose

159

Standing in
your
purpose
makes
you
limitless

Eliza Williams

Laconic Poetry & Prose

160

Your words are
spells
be careful
what you
speak
because
your
mind and body
will hold you to it

Eliza Williams

Laconic Poetry & Prose

161

Can you love me
winter
summer
spring
and fall
because there will
be off seasons
like football

Eliza Williams

Laconic Poetry & Prose

162

Can you love this tree
when I haven't a
leaf
Can you see
with
or
without
a leaf
I am still
the same tree

Eliza Williams

Laconic Poetry & Prose

163

Is that
summertime
passion
just a
fashion

Eliza Williams

164

I am grateful
I am patient
I am trusting
If I'm grateful
I am patient
If I am patient
I am trusting

I'm learning that
gratitude
patience
and
trust
are akin

Eliza Williams

Laconic Poetry & Prose

165

I love the
life outside
and inside
of me

Eliza Williams

166

I used to be a
caterpillar
but I underwent a
metamorphosis
that gave me the
most beautiful wings

Eliza Williams

Laconic Poetry & Prose

167

Your
actions
should
follow
your
words

Eliza Williams

168

There ain't no such
thing as half a sun
Either you showing up
or you ain't
Either it's daylight
or
night

Eliza Williams

Laconic Poetry & Prose

169

Warning:

When you ride your bike
You must watch out for
the
glass
nails
and
rocks
I didn't mention cars in the above
because I only ride in lanes
reserved for my bike

Eliza Williams

Laconic Poetry & Prose

170

It seems
I have run
out of excuses
and fear
I know heavy
abundance is
near

Eliza Williams

171

If we can play
together
we can
stay
together

Eliza Williams

172

Blessed am I
to have the
willpower
to bear
myself alone

Eliza Williams

173

Don't get
to comfortable
living a lie because
the truth will soon
prevail

Eliza Williams

174

These days the lines of
womanhood
and
manhood
are so blurred
The only
distinction
is body parts
Perhaps
that
has
always
been the only
distinction

Eliza Williams

Laconic Poetry & Prose

175

How poor does
your self worth have
to be if you
have to rely
on another
person's body
to
validate yourself

Eliza Williams

Laconic Poetry & Prose

176

The more I relinquish my
need to control things
the more I welcome
all of the universal
possibilities
working in my
favor

Eliza Williams

177

I want to add to someone's
happiness
I do not want to be
the source of their happiness

Eliza Williams

Laconic Poetry & Prose

178

We must become curious
about ourselves in the
way we are curious
about other people

Eliza Williams

Laconic Poetry & Prose

179

Consistency
begets
Consistency

Eliza Williams

Laconic Poetry & Prose

180

I miss touch so much but
I must steer clear of connections
that can't offer the
promise of longevity

Eliza Williams

181

If you hunt
when you are
full
then it's
only for
sport

Eliza Williams

182

There is
beauty in
"as is."

Eliza Williams

183

I don't always express
what I feel and observe
I usually wait
until I find balance
in my words

Eliza Williams

Laconic Poetry & Prose

184

If you are creating
something great
it cannot be done
in haste
Everything great
deserves grace

Eliza Williams

185

Soon I'll be
someone's
little
spoon

Eliza Williams

Laconic Poetry & Prose

186

Sometimes
I lie in
bed and
listen to the
sound
of
silence

Eliza Williams

187

I'm tired
of
holding things
Now I know what
Al Green meant when
he said "I'm so tired of
being alone, I'm
so tired of on my own."

Eliza Williams

Laconic Poetry & Prose

188

You don't experience
longing unless there is
someone out there with
whom you should
be belonging

Eliza Williams

189

My God I can't even
bear porn anymore
It sets me back and adds to
my overwhelming
urge to give myself

Eliza Williams

Laconic Poetry & Prose

190

NOTE TO SELF:

Help just means
you
don't
have to do
it alone
it does not mean you are
inadequate

Eliza Williams

Laconic Poetry & Prose

191

You can not know me
greater
than I know myself
for it is I
who sits with
the worst and greatest
parts of me

Eliza Williams

192

Nobody ever taught
me how to properly take
care of myself
but
I've literally been
out here taking care
of myself like
I've been
properly taught

Eliza Williams

193

If I like it
then it
does not
matter
who
doesn't

Eliza Williams

Laconic Poetry & Prose

194

Men don't lie to
women because women
can't handle the truth
They lie because they can't
handle the consequences
of their own truth

Eliza Williams

195

There is
always a
reason to
be
grateful

Eliza Williams

Laconic Poetry & Prose

196

Been feeling
the overwhelm
of not sharing myself
and
not being shared with

Eliza Williams

197

Suppression never comes
out in balanced ways
It is
always
EXTREME

Eliza Williams

Laconic Poetry & Prose

198

At my lowest
I sometimes
look my best
I often
wonder why is that

Eliza Williams

Laconic Poetry & Prose

199

When it rains
just remember
every living thing
on this planet would
die if it was not for
water
Your growth depends on water
You can't experience life without the rain
It's just nature

Eliza Williams

200

Sometimes I feel like
I'm dependable
but
there is no space
for me to depend

Eliza Williams

Laconic Poetry & Prose

201

I'm grateful for the people
I can depend on and those
who can depend on me
Interdependence is
so underrated

Eliza Williams

202

It is in my alone time
where I learn
just how equipped
I am to carry myself
Some of the most beautiful
parts of myself begin to
spill out all over me

Eliza Williams

Laconic Poetry & Prose

203

For 5 sessions
I left my 8 minute personalized
100 affirmations on repeat
I cried
breathed
smiled
all on beat
That night I experienced
The most immaculate sleep

Eliza Williams

Laconic Poetry & Prose

204

Finding your purpose
is the beginning
of unlocking
your freedom

Eliza Williams

Laconic Poetry & Prose

205

I like free thoughts
I like to free my thoughts
until I'm free of thoughts
Just me
and
my complete presence

Eliza Williams

206

I wrote a letter to man
in jail
Mama said "A letter in jail
to an inmate is love
It's like commissary
Made time to talk to my
Mom today

Eliza Williams

207

Lemonheads
now & laters
pickles in a bag
Van Holten's
Oatmeal Pies
Pickled Pig Feet
Watermelon flavored suckers
in the shape of a cut off piece of watermelon
Cherryheads
Appleheads
Devil Squares
You remind me of my childhood where
I had all the sour and saccharine I could eat
but no longer do I desire to eat the past
However I do have a hankering for
my future to be a treat

Eliza Williams

208

Of course I want love
but I want to be sure
that I'm not using love
to "distract" me from
my greater self

Eliza Williams

209

If you are present
you may come
to realize that
like water age
too is fluid

Eliza Williams

Laconic Poetry & Prose

210

Clothes are not indicative
of one's sexuality
However
I certainly behave
a lot different in
a dress than I do pants

Eliza Williams

211

Your memories
they can hunt you
even the good ones
You start longing for those nouns
a person
a place
a thing
You long for a time
But it is in this time that
you find that you must cling
to the present moment the most
Fortunately
it is all you have
everything will eventually dissolve to a memory

Eliza Williams

212

Are we fated
or
Are we faded
I don't want to wake up
jaded
dealing with hyper emotions
that keep me gated

Eliza Williams

213

I want to obsess
over me
without it bleeding over
into narcissism
To keep it truth
I want to care about
other people too

Eliza Williams

Laconic Poetry & Prose

214

Safety trumps sexuality
When you feel safe with someone
Sex can sometimes happen
regardless
of the anatomy

Eliza Williams

215

Nowadays women got
to protect themselves
because men are overly
concerned with their
hair
bags
and
nails
some even get BBL's
strange unavoidable details

Eliza Williams

216

When you done marching
and
crying about niggas dying
remember this system was NOT
designed for your kind

Eliza Williams

Laconic Poetry & Prose

217

I want
to be
opened
before
I
open

Eliza Williams

218

I have learned
over the years that money
is synonymous to time
It is not about how
much you have
it's about how
you spend it

Eliza Williams

Laconic Poetry & Prose

219

As a young girl
I've been the butt of
many jokes for not
being among those
with big ASSets
but frankly I do
fairly well without
the BBL
I guess all asses aren't
created equal

Eliza Williams

Laconic Poetry & Prose

220

I take
no issue
with polygamy
but one
woman
is enough

Eliza Williams

Laconic Poetry & Prose

221

Gratitude is such
an underrated
human experience

Eliza Williams

Laconic Poetry & Prose

222

I know "apostles"
that are imposters
May God
be
with them too

Eliza Williams

Laconic Poetry & Prose

223

Love is not to
be supressed
especially for yourself

Eliza Williams

224

Paramours that you
thought
were forever
yours
turned nevermores

Eliza Williams

Laconic Poetry & Prose

225

It is a fact
that I fantasize sex
more than I have it
I desire the reverse
And beyond that I want
sex exactly the way I fantasize

Eliza Williams

Laconic Poetry & Prose

226

Unsuccessful
paramours
can become the
catalyst to your
artistic growth

Eliza Williams

Laconic Poetry & Prose

227

Let's fuck
Friday
and
go to
yoga
on
Saturday

Eliza Williams

228

Alone has never
bothered me until
I didn't want to be
alone

Eliza Williams

229

Nowadays people don't
want to be alone, but they
don't know how to be
together

Eliza Williams

Laconic Poetry & Prose

230

We tell women
that they are worth less
when they have birthed a life/lives
It is apparent our society does not
respect motherhood but beyond
that they do not respect life

Eliza Williams

231

Yes
our society is painfully revolting
It does not respect the elderly
It "respects" the youth only so that
it can prey upon them and taint them
When a society does not respect the elderly
we are left with a whole generation of people
who do not look forward to "growing up"
Growing up is a natural part of life
It is a fact that your mind and appearance
will change
We have children who are unguided because
their parents have no desire to be "grown"

Eliza Williams

Laconic Poetry & Prose

232

Some men reserve romance
for men
and
sex for women
I'm just saying it how I've
seen it

Eliza Williams

233

When you have been
"the hand" it is so difficult
to ask for a hand

Eliza Williams

Laconic Poetry & Prose

234

I'll be your prophylactic use
me as you see fit

Eliza Williams

Laconic Poetry & Prose

235

Some words sound
better when they are written
Some words sound better when
they are spoken

Eliza Williams

236

I miss teams
Everybody had a
position of
importance

Eliza Williams

237

Have you ever
seen the stars
in Mississippi
The sky is a cluster
of unforeseen beauty
I heard it's better in Africa
but I have never been

Eliza Williams

Laconic Poetry & Prose

238

My bank account hit zero
I hit a mental low
Then I realized my
low was a luxury

Eliza Williams

Laconic Poetry & Prose

239

I smell the scent of you
even when you are not near
I see you even when you are not here
I remember the taste of your lips
I miss your stare
and the way it felt when
I rubbed and touched your hair
But alas
Our rhythms have changed
and
We can't seem to stay on beat
I hear your silence but I dare you to speak

Fliza Williams

Laconic Poetry & Prose

240

I see who you are
I see who you are not
I see who you so desperately want to be
I have no judgements about what I see
For you are human
We are all unique
And with that I have made my peace

Eliza Williams

Laconic Poetry & Prose

241

Hypnotize yourself with positivity
until the affirmations are affirmed

Eliza Williams

242

I have felt all that I am
and could have been
like
everything everywhere all at once
All of me is existing inside and outside
in multiple spaces like the multiverse
I guess I'm multi-versed

Eliza Williams

243

I often picture someone
there to escape the reality
of sometimes being alone

Eliza Williams

244

Race is like the equator
it's not real
but it's an imaginary line
that divides nonetheless

Eliza Williams

Laconic Poetry & Prose

245

Sometimes I self obsess
and I marvel at how
uniquely designed I am

Eliza Williams

Laconic Poetry & Prose

246

Oh
the disappointment you experience
after arriving at what you believe to be
"the ultimate" soulmate
only to discover that you missed
your intended exit and detoured

Eliza Williams

Laconic Poetry & Prose

247

Sexual freedom is so underrated
because nowadays people are having
a lot of sex that is simply NOT
freeing

Eliza Williams

Laconic Poetry & Prose

248

Sometimes I wonder if the kind
of lover I yearn for myself is only
reserved for that in which I
read
in
novels
hear in song
or
watch in movies on T.V.
Like do I lean too far into
my fantasies

Eliza Williams

Laconic Poetry & Prose

249

Self love involves no one
but yourself
It is a perfectly acceptable
selfish act
so that you may be self(full)

Eliza Williams

Laconic Poetry & Prose

250

Wasted energy = exhaustion
Be sure to give your energy to
things and people that contribute
to your revitalization and restoration

Eliza Williams

Laconic Poetry & Prose

251

Some people can only
commit to a moment
Perhaps
they can not see
a future
How can blame anyone
for being present

Eliza Williams

252

If someone tells
you that you deserve
better than them
you do

Eliza Williams

Laconic Poetry & Prose

253

Self love is such
revolutionary act

Eliza Williams

254

If "they" changed
today's standard of beauty
how attractive would you believe
yourself to be tomorrow

Eliza Williams

Laconic Poetry & Prose

255

I have learned that true
healing takes center stage
when you are aligned with your
life purpose

Eliza Williams

Laconic Poetry & Prose

256

Perfection is the real flaw

Eliza Williams

Laconic Poetry & Prose

257

Back when the sun was out
and I didn't have to be so inside
Back before covid so
heavily impacted our lives

Eliza Williams

258

Your low can be someone
else's high
so remember gratitude

Eliza Williams

Laconic Poetry & Prose

259

Sometimes people value you
less when you are always available
to them
especially
when they have a sorted history
of dealing with inaccessible people

Eliza Williams

Laconic Poetry & Prose

260

No one can
teach you how to
accept yourself
except yourself

Eliza Williams

Laconic Poetry & Prose

261

The problem with relationships
most people are looking for
someone to die with instead
of someone to live with

Eliza Williams

Laconic Poetry & Prose

262

People are a lot like vehicles
these days
they just aren't designed
to be classic anymore

Eliza Williams

263

I'm going to paint in my journal
I'm going to write on my canvas
I'm going to sing my poetry
I'm going to listen with my eyes
and see with my ears
And when I'm thirsty I'll drink my tears

Eliza Williams

Laconic Poetry & Prose

264

In order to climb you must
relinquish your fear of heights
In order to fly you must relinquish
your fear of flights

Eliza Williams

265

If they can keep you
consuming then they have
consumed you

Eliza Williams

Laconic Poetry & Prose

266

People say "get comfortable with
being uncomfortable"
I don't much agree with that statement
because I do the uncomfortable so that
I may be comfortable

Eliza Williams

Laconic Poetry & Prose

267

Your self worth is a matter of
your own assessment
whatever you decide to tell
yourself becomes your truth

Eliza Williams

Laconic Poetry & Prose

268

Met a self proclaimed fat boy who
said that he wasn't really fat
he was just filled with trauma
I felt that shit heavy
No pun intended
but there is a
big pun here

Eliza Williams

Laconic Poetry & Prose

269

Two Haikus

5 Eliza is Earth
7 On the water she will surf
5 Oh earth, what beautiful turf

5 The sea has shattered
7 Connection to earth matters
5 All over peace shatters

Eliza Williams

Laconic Poetry & Prose

270

Sometimes you
just have to do
what you can
and leave
everything else
up to chance

Eliza Williams

271

Some people think
too much about
whose against them
as oppose to whose
with them
What we think is
what we attract

Eliza Williams

272

I'm pro-life but I do uphold
the belief that all women deserve the right to choose

Eliza Williams

273

Misunderstanding someone's gender
expression based on their outward appearance
is NOT a direct correspondence to phobia
It is simply a misunderstanding
Let's understand

Eliza Williams

Laconic Poetry & Prose

274

Always remember when
you are going through the process
of growing oneself that whatever you are
doing it is enough
because "doing" is enough
Keep building and you will soon
have a liveable house

Eliza Williams

Laconic Poetry & Prose

275

As an artist I have experienced the feeling of
what I like to describe as an "impoverished affluence"

It's like I know I'm rich from an inherent internal
value and talent that breeds my intellectual property
but I am stifled by a set of circumstances that I must go
to war with before I can unlock my intended abundance

It's like that fucking reality show "Survivor." The contestants must go
through a series of challenges before they can win a million dollars
One wrong choice or move can be the end of the million dollars

It's like unlocking levels in a video game to earn more
you have more to work with but the levels are much
more difficult and you still have to keep from dying because
you don't want to repeat the same shit all over again

I said all of that to say

I'm leveling up despite how difficult my circumstances

I'm making the right choices, unlocking my abundance
and staying the fuck alive

Eliza Williams

276

Location: Near self actualization
Time: During inner work
Movement: Towards my highest state of being

Eliza Williams